Be Happy For Me

A Comedy

by Jerry Sterner

A Samuel French Acting Edition

FOUNDED 1830

New York Hollywood London Toronto

SAMUELFRENCH.COM

Copyright © 1987 by Jerry Sterner

ALL RIGHTS RESERVED

CAUTION: Professionals and amateurs are hereby warned that *BE HAPPY FOR ME* is subject to a Licensing Fee. It is fully protected under the copyright laws of the United States of America, the British Commonwealth, including Canada, and all other countries of the Copyright Union. All rights, including professional, amateur, motion picture, recitation, lecturing, public reading, radio broadcasting, television and the rights of translation into foreign languages are strictly reserved. In its present form the play is dedicated to the reading public only.

The amateur live stage performance rights to *BE HAPPY FOR ME* are controlled exclusively by Samuel French, Inc., and licensing arrangements and performance licenses must be secured well in advance of presentation. PLEASE NOTE that amateur Licensing Fees are set upon application in accordance with your producing circumstances. When applying for a licensing quotation and a performance license please give us the number of performances intended, dates of production, your seating capacity and admission fee. Licensing Fees are payable one week before the opening performance of the play to Samuel French, Inc., at 45 W. 25th Street, New York, NY 10010.

Licensing Fee of the required amount must be paid whether the play is presented for charity or gain and whether or not admission is charged.

Stock licensing fees quoted upon application to Samuel French, Inc.

For all other rights than those stipulated above, apply to: Samuel French, Inc.

Particular emphasis is laid on the question of amateur or professional readings, permission and terms for which must be secured in writing from Samuel French, Inc.

Copying from this book in whole or in part is strictly forbidden by law, and the right of performance is not transferable.

Whenever the play is produced the following notice must appear on all programs, printing and advertising for the play: "Produced by special arrangement with Samuel French, Inc."

Due authorship credit must be given on all programs, printing and advertising for the play. ë

No one shall commit or authorize any act or omission by which the copyright of, or the right to copyright, this play may be impaired.
No one shall make any changes in this play for the purpose of production.
Publication of this play does not imply availability for performance. Both amateurs and professionals considering a production are strongly advised in their own interests to apply to Samuel French, Inc., for written permission before starting rehearsals, advertising, or booking a theatre.
No part of this book may be reproduced, stored in a retrieval system, or transmitted in any form, by any means, now known or yet to be invented, including mechanical, electronic, photocopying, recording, videotaping, or otherwise, without the prior written permission of the publisher.

ISBN 978-0-573-69049-5   Printed in U.S.A.   #3981

BILLING AND CREDIT REQUIREMENTS

All producers of BE HAPPY FOR ME *must* give credit to the Author in all programs and in all instances in which the title of the Play appears for purposes of advertising, publicizing or otherwise exploiting the Play and/or production. The author's name *must* appear on a separate line in which no other name appears, immediately following the title of the play, and *must* appear in size of type not less than fifty percent the size of title type.

BE HAPPY FOR ME, by Jerry Sterner, directed by John Ferraro, with scenery by David Potts, costumes by Abigail Murray, lighting by Greg MacPherson, was presented by David C. Gold at the Douglas Fairbanks Theatre, N.Y.C. Opening Night: January 7, 1986.

CAST
(In order of appearance)

PHIL	David Groh
NORMAN	Philip Bosco
ELIZABETH	Priscilla Lopez
A BLACK JACK DEALER/CAB DRIVER	Russ Pennington

SETTING
Aruba, an island in the Caribbean

TIME
The present

Be Happy for Me

ACT ONE

SCENE 1

A beach. Sun and sand. Pause several beats.

NORMAN. (*offstage*) For Christ's sake — How much longer?
PHIL. (*offstage*) A few more yards.
NORMAN. (*offstage*) A few more yards we'll be in Bimini. Our hotel is in Aruba. (*PHIL enters* S.L., *jogging to* C.S. *PHIL is forty-three and attractive. He wears a brief bathing suit, under his jogging pants and a fashionable floral print shirt. He carries a beach chair on one shoulder and a fashionable leather bag on the other.*) A few more yards and the Giants would have beat the Colts in the '58 playoffs. (*NORMAN enters* S.L. *He clumsily carries a beach chair and umbrella. He wears a silly flowered beach costume along with shoes and socks. He wears a hat with a visor to keep the sun away. NORMAN is a pleasant-looking forty-nine, noticeably graying with a bit of a pot belly. He looks out of his environment and ridiculous. And he's tired.*) A few more yards and I'll be dead.
PHIL. (*putting his beach chair down*) This is it. We're here.
NORMAN. This?
PHIL. (*angling his chair to the sun*) Look at the ocean and the coastline. Gorgeous. You can see the hotel way back there.
NORMAN. Where's the lifeguard?
PHIL. There is no lifeguard.

NORMAN. No lifeguard? How can you swim in the ocean without a lifeguard? What about the undertow? Don't you remember what Mom taught us?

PHIL. Mom never came to the Caribbean.

NORMAN. We're the only two here.

PHIL. It's early.

NORMAN. It's not that early. If they had lifeguards they'd have people. (*PHIL takes off shirt revealing brief bathing suit.*) You're kidding.

PHIL. What?

NORMAN. What happened—did they shrink in the wash?

PHIL. No, they didn't shrink in the wash.

NORMAN. It was a bar mitzvah present?

PHIL. It wasn't a bar mitzvah present. I'm overdressed.

NORMAN. Overdressed? I got jockstraps bigger than that.

PHIL. Overdressed. This is a nude beach.

NORMAN. A nude beach! Really . . . I hope you don't think I'm . . .

PHIL. I love you. I really do. More than you know. (*PHIL moves to hug him. NORMAN gently pushes him away—a little uncomfortable*) This vacation was a great idea. Just the two of us. I'm really glad you thought of it.

NORMAN. Yeah. Come on. Let's get some sun.

PHIL. That's not like you. Something's up. You going to tell me now or later?

NORMAN. Is that the casino down there?

PHIL. I take it it'll be later.

NORMAN. Is that the casino?

PHIL. Ready to break the bank?

NORMAN. Why not?

PHIL. It's tough when you bet ten dollars a hand.

NORMAN. I'll win twelve in a row, I'll go to fifteen.

BE HAPPY FOR ME

Don't worry. When it comes to casinos I have the courage of an accountant. (*PHIL laughs, adjusts chairs, and lies down. NORMAN adjusts chair away from the sun. Their beach chairs form a "V" facing the audience.*)

PHIL. What are you doing?

NORMAN. What?

PHIL. The sun is this way.

NORMAN. I know. We see it in New York every so often. (*NORMAN lies down on his beach chair.*) How can you lie there and stare at the sun? You'll go blind.

PHIL. I don't stare at the sun. I keep my eyes closed. How else are you going to get your eyelids tanned?

NORMAN. Oh . . . that's how it's done.

PHIL. Sure, otherwise I wouldn't want to blink when I get home.

NORMAN. Yea . . . But how are you going to know when the naked girls get here?

PHIL. I'll smell them. (*begins taking out his suntan lotions and carefully sets them down*)

NORMAN. You're going to smell them through that?

PHIL. Malibu nose. Three marriages, four kids, five hundred affairs. Anybody could do it.

NORMAN. Time for a nose job . . . God it's hot. (*NORMAN gets up and goes to umbrella.*)

PHIL. What're you doing?

NORMAN. (*planting umbrella behind his chair*) It's too hot.

PHIL. Maybe if you took off your hat, shirt, shoes and socks you wouldn't be so hot.

NORMAN. I'm not taking off anything. This sun is vicious.

PHIL. When we get back to the hotel I'm buying you some thongs.

NORMAN. Can't wear them.

PHIL. Why?

NORMAN. That thing you put between your toes — it hurts.

PHIL. Only for a couple of hours. A callus forms and you're fine.

NORMAN. I'm too old to start breaking in my toes. They wouldn't understand.

PHIL. It's good I love you.

NORMAN. So where are all these naked girls?

PHIL. Hopefully, they won't show.

NORMAN. What do you mean?

PHIL. I'll be embarrassed. Look at the way you're dressed.

NORMAN. Look at the way they're dressed. They should be the ones embarrassed.

PHIL. Not on a nude beach.

NORMAN. I got the solution. We'll tell them we got our signals mixed up. We'll tell them I thought we were going to a ski lodge and this is my clubhouse outfit.

PHIL. I'll settle. Just take off your shoes and socks.

NORMAN. Shoes. Leave my socks alone. The sand is too hot.

PHIL. You're not on the sand. You're on the lounge.

NORMAN. And what happens when the naked girls get here? I can't just lie here and look up at them.

PHIL. Why not?

NORMAN. Because that's not the way we do things at Morgan Guaranty. I've got to stand up and introduce myself and the last thing I need then is hot feet.

PHIL. I've got news for you. If you don't take them off no one is coming over. They're not interested in meeting Santa Claus on the beach.

NORMAN. Ok. Ok. I'll take off my shoes and socks.

You do the introductions. Don't suggest any walks. A deal?

PHIL. A deal.

NORMAN. (*NORMAN starts taking off his shoes and socks.*) Tomorrow it's two weeks. We should be home sitting shiva.

PHIL. Sitting shiva is better in the Caribbean.

NORMAN. . . . Yeah.

PHIL. Everything is better in the Caribbean. (*NORMAN, his shoes and socks off, lies back down on lounge.*) Are you ok?

NORMAN. Yeah.

PHIL. Sure?

NORMAN. Yeah . . . How about you?

PHIL. I guess so. I never knew him. How old were we when Mom threw him out?

NORMAN. I was twelve. You were six.

PHIL. . . . Thirty-seven years ago?

NORMAN. When was the last time you saw him?

PHIL. His fiftieth birthday . . . you were there . . . when was it?

NORMAN. Twenty years ago. We flew out to Milwaukee to be with him. Didn't even ask us to stay over.

PHIL. (*He reaches out his hand between chairs.*) Come on . . .

NORMAN. What?

PHIL. Take my hand.

NORMAN. What is it with you? You just come from an EST seminar?

PHIL. Stop fucking around. Take my hand. I want to tell you something. (*NORMAN takes his hand.*) I never missed him 'cause I had you. You were my brother . . . my father . . . my friend. When Mom left us for what's his name . . . the guy with the dancing school in Miami?

NORMAN. Rolando.

PHIL. Rolando Vegas.

NORMAN. His real name was Milton Schwartz.

PHIL. Right. Mom found out later. Was she pissed. I only remember his moustache. (*laughing*) You know, when she went senile a few years ago it never really affected me. As far as I'm concerned she was always senile.

NORMAN. You used to fight with her a lot.

PHIL. She was crazy. Everybody fought with her a lot. Except you. You were always making peace. Between me and her. Between her and Pop. I remember nights they used to fight and I pulled the covers over my head and you used to go downstairs. "Mom, he might have a point. Pop, there's another way of looking at it." And it worked. They shut up.

NORMAN. Till the next night.

PHIL. Not the point. She had nicknames for us, remember? You were the "Great Conciliator."

NORMAN. She enjoyed saying it. It was the biggest word she knew. "My son, the conciliator."

PHIL. And I was "The Crazy."

NORMAN. "The Lunatic."

PHIL. "The Lunatic." Right.

NORMAN. Phil?

PHIL. (*lost in his thoughts*) . . . Yeah?

NORMAN. Can I have my hand back?

PHIL. No.

NORMAN. It's getting numb.

PHIL. I don't care.

NORMAN. I'm going to put on my shoes and socks.

PHIL. Why?

NORMAN. Because it won't make any difference what

I'm wearing. No girls are coming over to us holding hands. My feet are getting burned for nothing. (*PHIL lets go of his hand, gets up and paces.*)

PHIL. If you won't tell me what you have to tell me at least let me talk to you. What did we go away together for—girls?

NORMAN. It looks like we're in a lot of trouble.

PHIL. I'm going to talk to you whether you want to hear it or not.

NORMAN. Don't. I don't know if I'm ready. I mean it.

PHIL. Why? You know what I'm going to say?

NORMAN. Yes.

PHIL. You're wrong. You haven't got the faintest idea . . . How do you know?

NORMAN. I'm clairvoyant.

PHIL. I tell you?

NORMAN. Only when you get married, divorced or drunk.

PHIL. Then I'm due. The divorce should be final in a couple of weeks.

NORMAN. Save it till then.

PHIL. I'll admit you might have some idea, but you don't know.

NORMAN. Don't know? You're about to do an hour and a half on me winding up with "Now that Pop is dead and Mom is certifiably senile you thank God I'm still there—an island of stability in a sea of trauma, turmoil and change."

PHIL. . . . You're a tough guy to give a compliment to.

NORMAN. It's affectionately termed your "Rock of Gibraltar" speech.

PHIL. I would have said it better.

NORMAN. I know.

PHIL. I should . . . I rehearsed it for two days. I was going to start by telling you I'm going to be in *Who's Who* next year.

NORMAN. Really?

PHIL. You see . . . didn't know that. "Famed Hollywood Divorce Attorney" reads the caption. They actually came to interview me. When they asked, "What drove you to become a divorce attorney," I answered, "Self-defense." They didn't know what the hell I was talking about. (*NORMAN smiles; PHIL as well.*) You know what I'm talking about, mister? (*PHIL moves to NORMAN and into an emotional embrace.*) You always knew what I was talking about. Always. (*PHIL pulls away—choked.*)

NORMAN. Why couldn't you come to the funeral?

PHIL. Why? I was in . . . the middle of things . . . He meant shit to me. That's what I'm trying to tell you. Besides, you were there. You would handle it. You always do.

NORMAN. You coming to my funeral? Chances are I'll be there.

PHIL. Norm—I would do anything—I would kill for you. Remember at Hebrew School, if you were Orthodox, the first thing you did when you woke in the morning was say a prayer thanking God you weren't born a woman? You remember? . . . You got a prayer?

NORMAN. Yeah. I thank God I don't have to go to Hebrew School today.

PHIL. I have one too. I thank God you're here. I'd rather be with you here—in the sun—relaxed, together —than some freezing cemetery in Milwaukee burying somebody I never knew. You know what my greatest regret is? You never needed anything from me. Never needed money or advice or—you never even needed a divorce for Christ sake. The only guy I know—so help me the only guy I know—married to the same woman forty years.

NORMAN. Twenty-three years.

PHIL. Same thing. I think you're doing it out of spite.

NORMAN. Myra will be pleased to hear that.

PHIL. Trying to repay you has got to be the most frustrating experience of my life. I get the feeling if I became a butcher you'd become a vegetarian. But no more. Something's up. You finally need me.

NORMAN. I need the shade.

PHIL. I've been screaming for years, "Let's get away together—you and me." You always had some cockamamie excuse. You called me. Something's up. You need me. I'm ready.

NORMAN. I'm hot. I'm going back to the shade—if you don't mind.

PHIL. Mind? Do whatever you want. You want to fly to Milwaukee and freeze by the grave—we'll go. This vacation is yours. Whatever you want to do—wherever you want to sit, eat, sleep, meet—anything you want to do. In fact, you wanna put on your shoes and socks? (*NORMAN lies on lounge under umbrella. PHIL playfully attempts to put NORMAN's socks on.*) Come on. Come on. Put them on. It's ok. I don't mind.

NORMAN. The sand isn't as hot as I thought.

PHIL. That's because it's eight o'clock in the morning. God save me. Eight o'clock in the morning. Wait two hours. It'll get hot.

NORMAN. Maybe I'll put them on then. (*wiggling his toes*) Actually, it feels good like this.

PHIL. (*comes to him, pats him on the shoulder*) Watch out. Next comes the shirt and hat.

NORMAN. Never! . . . (*Phil lies down on his lounge.*)

Oh my God—Phil!

PHIL. (*alarmed*) What? What?

NORMAN. (*pointing away from PHIL*) A nude girl! I don't believe it. A nude girl! (*points*) Look!

PHIL. Don't point!

NORMAN. Phil—aren't you going to look? She's nude. Completely.

PHIL. Stop pointing. I'm not going to look.

NORMAN. Why not?

PHIL. Because it's not looking. It's staring.

NORMAN. What's the difference?

PHIL. When you look your tongue stays in your mouth. You'll go back with a sunburned tongue and toes—what will I tell Myra?

NORMAN. What do you want me do?

PHIL. Just stay calm. How far away is she?

NORMAN. Pretty far. About a hundred yards . . . she's walking along the water. Look.

PHIL. I'm not looking. Is she with anyone?

NORMAN. No. She's walking head down. Must be looking for sea shells. Where's she going to put them?

PHIL. All right, now listen. In a couple of seconds I'm going to sit up on the side of the chair and we're going to pretend to be engrossed in conversation. Ok? At the appropriate time I'll make eye contact with her. (*NORMAN shakes his head "Yes" vigorously.*) Ok. I'm going to do it now. (*He sits on side of chair facing NORMAN. NORMAN doesn't move. They both sit there several beats, NORMAN staring in the direction of the nude woman.*) Norman?

NORMAN. (*not moving*) Yes?

PHIL. How are we going to be absorbed in conversation if you don't look at me?

NORMAN. Phil, I hope she's not coming over here.

PHIL. That one?

NORMAN. Phil, I got a problem. I think I'm getting an erection.

PHIL. Oh my God, that's terrible.

NORMAN. I know. I know. Don't rub it in.

PHIL. Don't rub it in?

NORMAN. You know what I mean!

PHIL. Turn over on your stomach.

NORMAN. What, are you crazy — I'll kill myself.

PHIL. Christ . . . what are we going to do?

NORMAN. Listen. Listen. I'm going to pretend I'm asleep. If it goes away, I'll start to snore. You wake me up then, ok?

PHIL. If what goes away?

NORMAN. What?

PHIL. When you snore what goes away — the girl or the erection?

NORMAN. The erection. I won't know when the girl goes away. I'll be sleeping — got it?

PHIL. Got it. (*He waves to her.*)

NORMAN. Oh God — you made eye contact?

PHIL. Eye and arm. She waved back. Jesus, now she's jogging here. What a sight.

NORMAN. You think I should put my hat over it? (*PHIL leans over to look closer.*) Stop staring. You'll make it obvious.

PHIL. Doesn't look like it needs any help from me. I'm very impressed.

NORMAN. Oh God. Did you bring a camera?

PHIL. You want me to take a picture of it?

NORMAN. Not it. The girl. I'll be sleeping. I want to know what she looks like.

PHIL. You do? . . . When was the last time you had your eyes checked?

NORMAN. I don't know. Right now it's not my eyes I'm worried about.

PHIL. Sssh. She's almost here. Go to sleep. Hi. Good morning.

MALE VOICE. (*offstage*) Good morning. (*NORMAN stirs.*)

PHIL. Beautiful day, isn't it?

MALE VOICE. (*offstage*) Sure is. Your friend sleeping?

PHIL. Yes. He had a hard . . . we just arrived.

MALE VOICE. (*offstage*) Have a good day. See you later.

PHIL. Ciao! (*PHIL breaks up. NORMAN sits staring in the direction of the unseen person.*)

NORMAN. That was her? (*PHIL is hysterical.*) I can't believe it. I saw all that hair I . . .

PHIL. . . . Got all confused.

NORMAN. Well, it's hard to see in this goddamned sun. Always squinting. Will you control yourself? Will you please! (*PHIL tries his best. Satisfied, NORMAN continues.*) Did that guy have the longest hair and the littlest dick of anyone you ever saw? (*PHIL, hysterical once again, nods "yes".*) Why would a guy like that walk around like that?

PHIL. To make you crazy.

NORMAN. I'm crazy enough as it is.

PHIL. You — the Rock of Gibraltar!

NORMAN. That's right. I am the Rock of Gibraltar. I'm just there — inert. Life goes swirling all round me. I just sit there like a goddam rock.

PHIL. You want to bo back to the hotel and talk?

NORMAN. No, I don't want to go the hotel and talk. I want to stand here and yell. I want to scream.

PHIL. At Pop?

NORMAN. (*motioning offstage*) No. Not at Pop. At

that jerk. I would call him a prick if he had one.

PHIL. Why not Pop?

NORMAN. Stop that. Stop that shrink shit, Phil. Twenty years of shrinkage and you're beginning to sound like one. Pop is dead. It's over. He never was. Mom too.

PHIL. So?

NORMAN. So?

PHIL. So what's this all about — some guy with a little dick?

NORMAN. Exactly — it takes a hairy, mini-schlonged exhibitionist to point out just how ridiculous I am.

PHIL. You were never "ridiculous."

NORMAN. Don't bullshit me. You like "pathetic" better?

PHIL. I don't like either.

NORMAN. Really? What would you call someone who had one wife for twenty-three years, one job for twenty-five, and one address and phone number for twenty-two.

PHIL. Loyal?

NORMAN. Come on.

PHIL. Considerate?

NORMAN. To who? The post office? I read the average American family moves every 2.7 years. I have seen six mailmen retire on my route and I'm still going strong.

PHIL. If you're really looking for the "word" I have it. Try "successful." (*NORMAN laughs derisively.*) Let's start with the job. It's not one job. It's one company. Working your way up from shit to executive V.P., running a goddamned trust department portfolio worth hundreds of millions — that ain't chopped liver.

NORMAN. No. At Morgan Guaranty we call it paté.

PHIL. Don't play with me. They pay you six figures. They got to think you're pretty together.

NORMAN. You talk low, you take small bites, they

think you're together.

PHIL. That and outperform the Dow every year.

NORMAN. Outperforming the Dow is like kissing your sister. No big deal.

PHIL. You don't have a sister.

NORMAN. I have a million sisters. Do you know who I deal with? Do you have any idea? Dowagers. Their accountants and lawyers. Security analysts. Chartists.

PHIL. My ex-wives. (*NORMAN eases off, almost smiles.*) They love you.

NORMAN. 'Cause I've made them a few bucks.

PHIL. Even Liz is crazy about you.

NORMAN. How is she?

PHIL. Like always — pissed.

NORMAN. Why?

PHIL. She wanted to come with us. Listen, I don't want to talk about me or my third ex-wife. I want to talk about you.

NORMAN. Why didn't you say something? She could've come.

PHIL. I know she could have come. The whole idea was for us to be together. If Myra can understand she can understand.

NORMAN. Myra understands. Myra understands everything.

PHIL. What's that supposed to mean? Myra understands everything. I want to tell you something. There's not one woman I know — forget it — ever knew — that would let you go off like this. If Elizabeth were even one-tenth as understanding, we'd still be together . . . Maybe. Why are we talking about Elizabeth?

NORMAN. Because I don't want to talk about Myra.

PHIL. Aw shit. Oh no, Norm.

NORMAN. Don't carry on. There's no problem. Myra

is Myra. After twenty-three years, no more surprises. I don't want to talk about her now.

PHIL. Okay. But if I have to talk about Elizabeth, I have to lie down. Shrink's instructions. I generally become hysterical—my arms go flailing and my feet start kicking and I break half the things in his office. If I lie down it's better. (*He lies down, NORMAN sits next to him.*)

NORMAN. Why did she want to come.

PHIL. Why? Why? Because she's an actress without a job. Because she loves the sun. Because I'd be paying. Because it's her last chance to bust my balls. Because she's nuts. Because she's Elizabeth. Look at this, I'm getting worked up already.

NORMAN. I hope my being here didn't keep her . . .

PHIL. What, from coming? What are you talking about—she's crazy about you.

NORMAN. Come on.

PHIL. Come on yourself. I told you she's crazy about you and the family. Remember, early on, just after we were married and the kids met her? I forget whether it was Susan or Rachel—Susan, I think—called her Aunt Liz.

NORMAN. Tanta Liz.

PHIL. Right. Tanta Liz. Changed her whole image. Went around calling herself Tanta Liz. Even put on a bra a couple of days. (*NORMAN laughs—enjoying it.*) Calls you "Normal", for the only normal person she knows.

NORMAN. Yeah.

PHIL. And she never stops talking about her goddamn stocks—you remember I told her to give you a couple of bucks to invest. Just after we married.

NORMAN. Of course I remember. It was thirty-five grand.

PHIL. Well—you wouldn't believe it. She waits for

that statement every month like it's an alimony check—keeps a graph to chart her progress.

NORMAN. Good for her.

PHIL. Anyway, she won't touch it. A couple of years ago, she wanted me to get her a Jaguar—after all, the Mercedes and Caddy didn't express her properly. A Jaguar did. I told her to sell some stock and buy one. You thought I was asking her to do porno movies.

NORMAN. You remember I took her one day on a tour of the Stock Exchange. I'll never forget her reaction. We were on that catwalk overlooking the trading floor. She just gasped, "All those people chasing all that money." She said that it looked like a giant crap table. She was so excited.

PHIL. Yeah. Life to her is a giant crap table. Except she doesn't know how to play. Always betting the "come line." And always crapping out.

NORMAN. I'm sorry it didn't work.

PHIL. Me too. I could've used a win. You know when it was best? When we came to New York. That was always the best for us. Being with you and Myra and the Kids. No pressure. We were able to relax.

NORMAN. I looked forward to those visits.

PHIL. It never had a chance. She's so fucking crazy. You know what she wants me to do now? She wants me to sue the lawyer who represented her on our pre-nuptial agreement.

NORMAN. Shouldn't surprise you. It's your personality she objects to—not your legal ability.

PHIL. What are you talking about? *I* represented her on the pre-nuptial. She wants me to sue myself and get her a better deal. (*NORMAN laughs.*) I know—very funny—except when you live it.

NORMAN. At least you lived it. You followed your

heart. There are worse things.

PHIL. I didn't follow my heart. I followed my dick. There are no worse things.

NORMAN. Trust me. There are.

PHIL. Yeah. There are. Not ever knowing the difference. Worse than that. Knowing there is no difference.

NORMAN. Try talking low and taking small bites.

PHIL. So that's it. That's what you were trying to tell me. I should have known. Jesus Christ, you had me worried. (*laughs, kisses his brother on the cheek*) Male menopause. Happens every day. No biggie. In California it happens to guys in their twenties. (*doing push-ups as he talks*) Happened to me too, you know. After the second one. God, I thought that was going to be forever.

NORMAN. Your second wife's name was Vanessa.

PHIL. Ok. Vanessa. Right after that. Not only menopause — worse — impotence. Known in some quarters as terminal menopause. Not that I ever stopped seeing women. I'm a sociable guy. But came time in the relationship for — I was very mature. I'd sit them down, explain my problem, tell them that ordinarily I'd love to but I didn't wish to cause them or myself any discomfort or embarrassment. Good? The right thing to do?

NORMAN. The right thing to do.

PHIL. It was unbelievable. Women are weird. They get turned on by problems.

NORMAN. Opportunities.

PHIL. Right. It either brings out their maternal or masochistic instincts. I don't even know if they know which. Anyway — nothing. Flab city. My shrink is unconcerned — to him it's not a problem — it's a manifestation. He only deals with problems. I now accept the fact that I will remain celibate the rest of my life. I tell myself it's not the worst thing in the world. It's not cancer. And I've had my share. More than my share. I figure you're born with only so many shtups—I took mine early. I am resigned. Enter Liz. You got to be a moron not to know she's a turn-on and she likes me too and—I do the speech.

NORMAN. How did she react?

PHIL. Very strange. Most women did the "Aw, poor baby" routine. They would ask this or that. About the marriages—about my feelings. They found more questions—

NORMAN. Elizabeth never asked.

PHIL. Never. I do the speech while we're out having dinner. She gets up, takes my car keys and drives me to her place. Doesn't say a word. We go in, she points to the bed and goes into the bathroom. Not unusual. All women go into the bathroom. I get into bed—under the sheets—and start playing with myself so maybe I can look at least half-assed respectable when she comes out. Thirty seconds maybe, out she comes wearing nothing but this softball jersey with the number 8 on it.

NORMAN. Yogi Berra's number!

PHIL. Except she looked a lot better in it than Yogi ever did. She comes out determined—like it was an audition and this was a part she was after.

NORMAN. It was a part she was after.

PHIL. Walks over—stands above me—rips off the sheet. Scared the shit out of me. I go from flabby to non-existent in two seconds. It actually disappears—goes underneath the skin—you don't want to hear the rest of this, do you?

NORMAN. Sure. Why?

PHIL. Well . . . you weren't in the mood for my "Rock of Gibraltar" story. I didn't think you had time for this nonsense.

BE HAPPY FOR ME

NORMAN. It's ok. Go ahead.

PHIL. You're sure? You're not going anywhere? You got time?

NORMAN. Will you stop fooling around? Come on!

PHIL. Ok. So there she is — standing above me — rips off the sheet — down it goes — she laughs and points to it.

NORMAN. To where it was.

PHIL. To where it was, And you know what she says?

NORMAN. What?

PHIL. "Come out. Come out. Wherever you are." (*NORMAN laughs, PHIL too.*) I figured, "Well, there goes another five years with the shrink." Right? But then the most amazing thing happened. It began to re-emerge. Not a lot — a little. Like a turtle sticking his head out from under the shell — checking out the scene. Encouraging, but it was still touch and go. Then she ripped off old number 8 and points, "I see you. You're it." Doesn't talk to me. Plays hide and seek with it. Like I had an air pump in my stomach it springs to attention. It looked at it — filled with wonder — maybe like a woman must feel when she's giving birth — "Is that part of me? Did I do that?" Being a man of the world and very together — you know what I said?

NORMAN. What?

PHIL. "Don't get excited. It won't stay." Would you believe it? For the first time since she's in the room she looks at me and you know what she says? "Are you kidding — piece of cake." Goodbye, menopause — Hello, insanity!

NORMAN. No further problems?

PHIL. (*lies on sand and begins push-ups*) Nope. Cured. Complete and total. I'm going to cure you too.

NORMAN. I'm not impotent.

PHIL. I know. I saw. So . . . you want to know the cure?

NORMAN. I want to know the disease.

PHIL. Disease? It's called death. Now that Pop is gone there's nothing between you and the grave but time. You want me to "go with it"? That's Californian for "elaborate." (*NORMAN doesn't respond.*) First you're born, then you marry and become a father, then you're a grandfather—then you die. And that's if you're lucky.

NORMAN. What's my present heading—"latent grandfather"?

PHIL. Actively latent. I saw Susan before she left for school, remember?

NORMAN. Oh God, Phil—my kids have had more sexual experiences than me.

PHIL. Come on. Don't let's get carried away.

NORMAN. It's true. In my whole life I've had two women. One—twice!

PHIL. Well . . . You're probably right.

NORMAN. Don't agree so fast. Susan, I know—Rachel is still a virgin.

PHIL. How old is she?

NORMAN. Sixteen.

PHIL. It's statistically possible.

NORMAN. What the hell is that supposed to mean? It's statistically possible at eighty. Rachel is still a virgin, goddamnit!

PHIL. I was joking. I know she is. Why are you?

NORMAN. Why am I what?

PHIL. A virgin.

NORMAN. I am not a virgin. I'm a neophyte. The distinction might be minor, but it's all I got.

PHIL. Good. Why don't you do something about it?

NORMAN. Like what?

PHIL. Like why not go out and have an affair like a normal married man.

NORMAN. Nobody ever offered.

PHIL. They won't if you don't send out the right signals.

NORMAN. What signals do you sent to "dowagers"?

PHIL. The same signals you send to secretaries, file clerks, waitresses, everybody. It's like when the "Dow" sends out a buy signal. We're at a new high, all's well with the world, buy buy buy buy. You send out your fuck signal—I'm here, I'm fun, I'm ready. Fuck fuck fuck fuck fuck.

NORMAN. You . . . are going through menopause. (*muttered*) Fuck fuck fuck fuck . . .

PHIL. Are you telling me they don't have affairs at Morgan Guaranty?

NORMAN. I don't know. If they do it's so discreet it's not worth having.

PHIL. Discreet? They come to California, those pasty-faced assholes, they walk around with their tongues hanging out and their hands in their pockets.

NORMAN. Like me.

PHIL. Like you. Like me. Like everybody. Because it's what we want. It's the cure.

NORMAN. Getting laid is the cure?

PHIL. Yes. Yes.

NORMAN. For what?

PHIL. For everything! Getting laid is like a great vacation. No matter how it goes you think about it before and you remember it after. And we're always ready to take a vacation.

NORMAN. Not after this conversation.

PHIL. It's the cure. It's exactly what you need. I promise. It's exciting. It clears out your nasal passages. It puts you back emotionally to when you were a kid. Your heart goes pitter pat and your hands get sweaty and—

NORMAN. In New York, they call that anxiety.

PHIL. It's called being alive. It's looking forward to something other than your Keogh Plan and the next move in the Dow.

NORMAN. (*sarcastically*) "Going for it."

PHIL. You're goddamn right. Going for it.

NORMAN. Great. Go for it. Have an affair. Makes you feel like twenty. Pitter pat, pitter pat. Hang in two—three years. Christ—approaching thirty. Let's get out. Go for it again. Pitter pat, pitter pat. Look at this . . . twenty again. Ain't life grand when you're eternally young? Except one day you'll forget to do your push-ups or take your yeast or hemoglobin or whatever the hell those things are and you'll wake up. And look at this—from a teenager to an old man in eight restful hours—God's little way of saying, "Boogah—boogah." And the lady lying next to you will scream, grab the kids and disappear. And you'll be all alone with ex-wives, ex-lovers, ex-kids spread all across this great land like little procreating fruitflies. And you won't even know your goddamn mailman.

PHIL. . . . Procreating fruitflies? Give me a break. Norman, my only mistake is, I marry them. And I don't want to know my mailman. You know enough for both of us.

NORMAN. (*pauses several beats*) Pop's death did shake me. A lot. You're right, there's nothing between me and the grave but time. Predictable time. The only surprises left will be unpleasant ones. The night I heard Pop died, all I could see was this tombstone that read "He consistently outperformed the Dow."

BE HAPPY FOR ME

PHIL. Very subtle. No shrink is going to get rich from you.

NORMAN. The next morning I didn't go to work. I totalled up all of our investments—figured out how much it was worth. Do you realize I can live without working for the rest of my life? (*PHIL rises, hand outstretched, and shakes his brother's hand.*)

PHIL. Fantastic!

NORMAN. I can't live extravagantly. But I can live decently.

PHIL. That's really great. Of course it's a lot easier when you're not exactly a spender.

NORMAN. Making it was the easy part. The hard part is—now what do you do?

PHIL. You know?

NORMAN. Yes.

PHIL. . . . So?

NORMAN. Remember when we were kids, Phil? For our birthdays? Mom always got us this chocolate layer cake.

PHIL. Yeah, sure. With hard icing. Great cake.

NORMAN. Remember what we did with it?

PHIL. We ate it.

NORMAN. Remember how?

PHIL. Why are we talking about chocolate cake?

NORMAN. You used to eat all the icing first.

PHIL. It was the best part. After the icing I used to eat the cream between the layers. Still do.

NORMAN. I used to save the icing for last. The best for last.

PHIL. Half the time when you weren't looking Mom and me used to swipe it. You never got it.

NORMAN. I know.

PHIL. Norm . . . you retiring for chocolate cake?

NORMAN. Phil, I want to learn to play the banjo.

PHIL. Now you're talking sense. That's worth retiring for. Who knows? Later you'll learn to finger paint — refinish furniture . . .

NORMAN. And I want to fall in love. (*PHIL laughs.*) I'm serious, Phil. What you were talking about. The pitter pat. I want that feeling. I want to wake up excited. I want to remember that joke so I can tell it to her. I want to want to do push-ups and drink hemoglobin so I can look terrific. And I want to fall in love. That's what I want. (*PHIL shakes his head.*) I want to fall in love. For one time in my life, Phil, for one time in my life, I want to feel what the poets feel.

PHIL. The poets?! The poets feel like shit. They're out on street corners spouting for quarters — from guys like you. And they're liars. They never tell you it's temporary.

NORMAN. Everything is temporary. I see them out there. Those lucky few in love. They walk different. They talk different. They become different.

PHIL. They become crazy.

NORMAN. They become alive.

PHIL. Until it ends. The love goes but the craziness stays.

NORMAN. I'm prepared to take that chance. I need to. I won't live the rest of my life without it. I want to fall in love.

PHIL. You don't. All you want is the icing on the cake. You're entitled.

NORMAN. Phil, listen. It's English — I'll do it slow. I . . . want . . . to . . . fall . . . in . . . love.

PHIL. Go out and get laid. Go out and have an affair.

NORMAN. I don't want an affair. I want a love affair.

Tell me how can I have a love affair without being in love?

PHIL. You cannot have a love affair without being in love. You also cannot have a love affair without first having an affair. And it's hard to have an affair without getting laid. It happens to be one of the essential ingredients. You have to start at the beginning.

NORMAN. I didn't know that was the beginning.

PHIL. It is. It is because that might be enough. For a lot of people it is.

NORMAN. Not for me. I want to be in love!

PHIL. (*screaming*) You are in menopause and I love you and you are hysterical! And I am crazier than you for even taking this seriously. Two women in forty-nine years — one twice — and you talk about falling in love. You can't even make it with a dowager. And I'm getting upset. This is going to be some vacation — you're in menopause and I'm having a nervous breakdown.

NORMAN. Are you goading me? Is this a tactic? I can't make it with a dowager? I can't?

PHIL. It's also possible I'm in menopause and you're having the nervous breakdown.

NORMAN. For your information, at Morgan Guaranty we don't make dowagers. We make dowagers money. A subtle but important distinction. And I probably could've gotten "laid" as you put it if I was looking for it.

PHIL. Like before. Go into a fetal position with your hands on your dick. (*mimicking his brother*) "Wake me when it's over, Phil." (*NORMAN stares, in silent rage.*)
. . . I'm sorry. (*NORMAN takes off his beach hat and throws it on the sand, rips off his shirt and flings it to the sand.*) What're you doing?

NORMAN. (*lying down on beach chair*) Getting a tan. I want to look good when we get laid tonight. Pass me the jellies. (*Slowly PHIL hands him some sunbathing lotion.*) Don't look at me like that. A tan in the afternoon. A screw in the evening. One easy motion. I say I need to fall in love. You say I need to get laid. I accept your position. I'm willing to try it.

PHIL. You're serious?

NORMAN. (*splashing lotion all over himself*) Yes, I'm serious. I'm getting laid tonight. I expect you to help me.

PHIL. Put it in the same place you put it in with Myra.

NORMAN. Ok. Don't help me. I'll just do it myself.

PHIL. All right, we're going to get so laid.

NORMAN. Tonight.

PHIL. Don't count on tonight. It's our first night here.

NORMAN. Tonight!

PHIL. We'll meet them tonight. Have a drink. Set it up. Nice and easy. Tomorrow we'll — get laid. Slow but sure.

NORMAN. Not this vacation. Not tomorrow. Tonight! Phil, my whole life is a testament to deferred gratification. What Job is to suffering I am to deferred gratification. (*he rises, runs to umbrella and throws it to the ground.*) I spent my whole life in the shade. I want the sun. (*He walks back to chair.*) Is this really a nude beach? (*He reaches for his bathing trunks. Begins to take them off . . .*)

BLACKOUT

SCENE TWO

TIME: *That evening.*
SETTING: *NORMAN and PHIL's hotel room. A bed has been added to the stage. It has a large headboard with a shelf for PHIL's lotions, potions, vitamins, etc.*

At each side is a small table. There is also a phone, an ashtray, and a light switch. Phil enters, half dressed. He continues dressing and primping through the top of the scene.

PHIL. You through with the bathroom?
NORMAN. (*offstage*) Yes. I'll be right out.
PHIL. C'mon already. Quit primping! We're going to kill 'em tonight! I'm looking forward to it. We'll dazzle them. You and me. Like in the old days.
NORMAN. (*offstage*) We never dated in the old days.
PHIL. But we dazzled them coast to coast. Tonight will be a picnic. You saw them out on the beach today — dozens of them. It's like going fishing only here they stock the pond.
NORMAN. (*offstage*) I think they're very young. I'm not sure. I never got up to their faces.
PHIL. That's the best part. Their eyes are so clear, their teeth are so white, skin so smooth. They're eager and attentive and easily impressed. And their bodies . . . !
NORMAN. (*offstage*) Stop already! I don't want to leave the game on the dressing room floor. (*NORMAN enters* S.R. *He is wearing a charcoal suit, black laced shoes, a white shirt and a maroon tie.*)
NORMAN. So? What do you think? (*He presents himself to his brother.*)
PHIL. I thought you wanted to get laid — not buried.
NORMAN. What's wrong? Too conservative?
PHIL. For everything but death. Take off your jacket.
NORMAN. Do I have enough cuff showing? (*He thrusts his arms out.*)
PHIL. I'm not going unless you take it off.
NORMAN. It's my favorite outfit.
PHIL. (*as he exits*) And the tie, too. (*NORMAN reluc-*

tantly begins taking off his tie and jacket. PHIL returns with a maroon sports jacket.) Try it on. Maybe it'll fit you. It's big on me.

NORMAN. It's red.

PHIL. It's maroon.

NORMAN. It's red. I never wore red.

PHIL. You never had an affair either. Put it on. (*Reluctantly, he lets PHIL put on the jacket.*) Not bad. Just don't button it.

NORMAN. My cuffs don't show. (*PHIL unbuttons NORMAN's top shirt button.*) What're you doing? (*He unbuttons several more, adjusts the cuffs.*) . . . If you bring out gold chains —

PHIL. You have any other shoes?

NORMAN. I have my browns. I'm big on earth tones.

PHIL. Like this? With laces?

NORMAN. Of course.

PHIL. Take off your shoes. (*NORMAN does. PHIL exits and returns holding a pair of maroon suede loafers with elevated heels.*)

NORMAN. Never. Never. Little elves wear things like that.

PHIL. Big elves too — when they're looking to score.

NORMAN. All right, all right. (*NORMAN begins changing shoes. PHIL continues dressing.*) Well, coach, any last minute advice?

PHIL. Don't mention Myra, the kids or the Dow.

NORMAN. What if I'm asked?

PHIL. You don't know what's going to happen to the Dow.

NORMAN. I'm not going to lie about it.

PHIL. It's not a lie. It's the truth.

NORMAN. I'm serious.

PHIL. I'm serious too. Tell them what you want. I'd tell

them I was separated. It's true. Myra is in New York and you're here. How much more separated can you get?

NORMAN. I'm not going to do that.

PHIL. Just play it by ear. You'll know what to do when the time comes. C'mon, stand up. Let's see how you look. (*NORMAN stands. PHIL looks him over, makes some minor last minute adjustments.*) Not bad. In my bedroom is a full-length mirror. Take a look.

NORMAN. I don't want to know. I look down now and wonder whose feet are walking my body.

PHIL. You look great. You got a little sun. We're going to kill them tonight. Believe me.

NORMAN. I believe you. I believe you.

PHIL. I want you to be excited. That's part of the fun. A big part.

NORMAN. I'm excited. I'm excited. Let me ask you — among young people, is there an . . . "in" position?

PHIL. An "in" position?

NORMAN. Sexual position?

PHIL. All positions are "in" positions — ultimately.

NORMAN. I mean a popular sexual position.

PHIL. (*laughs*) I love you.

NORMAN. What about the position?

PHIL. It's the first time. Don't get fancy.

NORMAN. Fancy? I'm just trying to survive.

PHIL. Unless she indicates a preference I would go with the traditional "male superior."

NORMAN. "Male superior"?

PHIL. Man on top. You can't get into trouble that way. If you go a second round I'd suggest, for a contrasting view and angle, female superior facing south.

NORMAN. Female superior — facing south? (*PHIL nods. NORMAN exits to beach, looks intently at the sky.*)

PHIL. By facing south I mean facing your feet.

NORMAN. I always face my feet.

PHIL. Not you — her! (*NORMAN tries to visualize. He does, gets despondent.*) Don't worry about it. You'll know what to do when the time comes.

NORMAN. Will you stop saying that? It sounds like I'm walking to my death — "when the time comes." It's almost eight. We've been up since dawn. I'm exhausted. We'll be here another four days. You were right. We got time. Maybe we should stay in. Order something from room service.

PHIL. (*mimicking NORMAN*) "Not this vacation. Not tomorrow. Tonight."

NORMAN. I had too much sun.

PHIL. (*reaches into drawer and takes out pills*) Take one of these.

NORMAN. What are they?

PHIL. No big deal. It revs you up a little. It'll put a Porsche engine in your Chevrolet body. (*PHIL takes one capsule, swallows it, hands on to NORMAN.*)

NORMAN. No water? You swallowed it like a veteran. You do this a lot?

PHIL. Don't be big brother. Take it.

NORMAN. I need water. (*PHIL hands him a glass of water.*) It won't make me impotent?

PHIL. I promise. No bad effects. If you're not used to it you'll talk a little more. That's it.

NORMAN. (*swallows, taking the whole glass to do so*) . . . I don't feel any different.

PHIL. See.

NORMAN. You know, we didn't have anything to eat all day. You figure if it's going to work it should work right away. I mean, it's going to hit that bloodstream like a ton of bricks. Bammo. But I don't feel any different.

PHIL. I told you.

NORMAN. I'm still a little nervous — but I was before

and I should be. Twenty-three years. But I'm excited too. Like just before you go on a roller coaster. Don't blame the pills, Phil. It's me. I have a very strong will. Those things don't work on me. Do you know I can't be hypnotized? Can't. Three guys tried. Couldn't. Couldn't get hypnotized. Tried and tried. I'm a bad subject. But you know what? I like that about me. I wouldn't want to be a "good subject." Why can't I stop talking? I can stop. Of course I can stop . . . See, I stopped. It wasn't long but I stopped. I wonder if my coordination is affected? Norman — hand left. (*His hand moves left.*) Norman, hand right. (*His hand moves right.*) I think I'm ok, but I can't stop talking. Oh God, Phil, what am I going to do?

PHIL. (*dressed, looks good*) We're leaving.

NORMAN. So soon? Wait a few minutes. What's the rush? Let's talk. Hey listen, how do you like this line for the right moment. "I may not be sexy but I'm comfortable." Huh? You like it? "I may not be sexy but I'm comfortable."

PHIL. I'm leaving.

NORMAN. Jesus, Phil, you're so impatient. (*PHIL exits. NORMAN pauses, looks about.*) And I want to correct something. The feeling I'm talking about — it's not just before — it's when you're already on the roller coaster, at the top of that first big hill — hardly moving — looking down — waiting — That incredible anticipation — excitement mixed with dread — that's the feeling! (*moves to exit*) It's a wonderful feeling . . . Phil — wait up. I'm coming.

(*He exits. Pause for several beats on the empty stage. We hear loud banging on the unseen door. ELIZABETH strides briskly onstage. She is about forty. Very attractive. Nice figure. She carries one piece of luggage. A cigarette dangles from her lips — she's always smoking.*)

ELIZABETH. Phil, you son-of-a-bitch. Where the hell are you! (*She slams down her suitcase.*)

CURTAIN

ACT TWO

Scene 1

TIME: *Several hours later.*
SETTING: *Hotel room and beach. As before. The stage is very dark. We hear off in the distance NORMAN and PHIL doing "You better watch out. You better not pout. You better not shout I'm telling you why, Santa Claus is coming to town." PHIL does most of the singing while NORMAN accompanies him on his fantasy banjo. They are dressed as we left them in the prior act.*

NORMAN. Stop. This is a very tough tune for the banjo. I think I'll need a few more lessons.
PHIL. You were terrific. Smooth. Funny. Like you've been fooling around for fifty years.
NORMAN. I always thought fooling around was tickling somebody. This is definitely better. It's those pills. They're terrific. Who make them? Let's go out and buy the stock.
PHIL. It's not the pills. It's you. You old smoothie.
NORMAN. I don't know how smoothie I am. I think I missed a few things.
PHIL. Like what?
NORMAN. Like if I was so smoothie why are we here and our friends back there?
PHIL. . . . You did miss a few things.
NORMAN. It's entirely possible. I was probably talking when it happened. Tell me.
PHIL. Our little friends from Fresno are waiting in their room.
NORMAN. For us?

PHIL. For you and me, babe. They wanted a few minutes to giggle and gargle. We sent champagne to their room. We're going to wash up, pack a toothbrush, and . . .

NORMAN. And?

PHIL. And?

NORMAN. And?

PHIL. And fuck our brains out! (*They sing, "Yes sir, that's my baby." Liz enters* U.L. *also singing. NORMAN, first into the room, stumbles over ELIZABETH's luggage and goes crashing to the floor. LIZ turns on the lights. NORMAN lies face down.*)

NORMAN. I'm o.k. Just keep singing.

PHIL. What are you doing here?

LIZ. A duet. C'mon, it's tough alone. "Yes sir, that's my baby . . ."

PHIL. I'm not singing with you. I'm not doing anything with you.

LIZ. "No sir, don't mean maybe . . ."

PHIL. I'm not. Our song is over. Finished.

LIZ. "Yes sir, that's my baby, now."

PHIL. What the hell are you doing here? I told you I didn't want you to come. Get out of here, you're boring.

LIZ. Boring? You want to hear boring? Pre-nuptial agreements are boring. Shyster lawyers are boring. (*NORMAN, unnoticed by them, begins regaining consciousness.*)

PHIL. Will you stop it!

LIZ. Take it back.

PHIL. Ok. I'll take it back. You're not boring, you're crazy. All right?

LIZ. All right. I can live with "crazy."

PHIL. You can? You do.

LIZ. I did.

PHIL. Can't run away from yourself, baby.

LIZ. (*pretending to write*) Can't — run — away — from — your —

PHIL. Get out of here! Get lost! Disappear!

LIZ. How come you don't return my phone calls? . . . Answer me.

PHIL. 'Cause I don't want to talk to you.

LIZ. Don't want to talk to me — who do you think you are? Since when did you become such a big shot?

PHIL. I'm going to be in *Who's Who* next year.

LIZ. Bravissimo. Then maybe you could tell me "what's what" with my checkbook — shit head! (*LIZ throws her checkbook at him. He ducks. It misses. PHIL crawls over to pick it up. She moves off bed toward PHIL.*) How come, shyster? How come?

PHIL. How come what?

LIZ. How come I'm overdrawn five grand — huh? How come I'm broke?

PHIL. You're broke?

LIZ. What do you think this is all about? You think I want to travel half way around the world to be with you?

PHIL. You're here 'cause you're broke?

LIZ. No. I'm here because cigarettes are cheaper.

PHIL. How did you get the money to come?

LIZ. I charged it — to you. You have the nerve not to return my calls.

PHIL. (*attempting to get control of himself, chokes a little on the cigarette*) Now let me tell you something. You are no longer my responsibility — my obligation. I don't know why you're broke —

LIZ. You lying son-of-a-bitch.

PHIL. I don't.

LIZ. You do.

PHIL. I don't.

NORMAN. I do. (*They stop and notice him for the first time. He sits on floor, back against dresser, checkbook open in his hands, still a little groggy.*) I think I do.

LIZ. Semi-conscious he has more brains than you. I had to pick the wrong brother. I pick men like I pick parts—shit.

NORMAN. (*to PHIL*) What was your settlement number?

LIZ. Sixty grand.

NORMAN. You make the payment?

PHIL. The first of the month.

LIZ. Liar! If you did I wouldn't be overdrawn.

PHIL. Why don't you shut up.

NORMAN. Sssshhh. Let's stay with the problem. Phil, did you make a sixty thousand dollar deposit?

LIZ. Of course he didn't. Then he would have been a man of his word. Then I would have money in the bank.

PHIL. You are sick. You are really sicker than I thought. Sixty grand payable $5000 monthly. I deposited $5000.

LIZ. Never. We never agreed to that.

PHIL. Never agreed. You didn't want it monthly. You wanted it every 26 days—blood money you called it. You even had your gynecologist send me your goddamned chart so you could be sure to get my check at the appropriate time. Sound familiar? (*LIZ is shaken.*) . . . What's the matter, big mouth, got nothing to say? Come on, come one, say something . . .

LIZ. I have nothing to say to you. I came to be with my friend. (*looking at NORMAN*)

PHIL. (*laughs derisively*) Your friend. Him? Ha!

LIZ. He is. I always wound up talking to him.

PHIL. Because I asked him to. Because you would never listen to me. Because, somehow, every once in a while he could get through to you. He was doing me a favor.

Liz. He's my best friend.

Phil. Only because of me. He happens to be friends with all my exes.

Liz. (*to NORMAN*) Are you my best friend?

Phil. He's mine. The marriage is over. He came with me and he leaves with me. Now get out!

Liz. I just want to stay the night. I'll leave in the morning.

Phil. No! Go get a cab. There's other places.

Liz. They're all sold out. I have no place to go.

Norman. Let her stay.

Phil. No. This is our vacation. She'll ruin it.

Norman. She said she'd leave in the morning.

Phil. Normie . . . All right, just the night. (*to LIZ*) Don't get carried away. (*to NORMAN*) I'll be waiting at the bar. Don't forget my toothbrush. (*to LIZ*) I'll be back in the morning. If you're still here I'll have you arrested for trespassing. (*He exits. LIZ crosses to exit and yells after him.*)

Liz. You're really scaring me, shithead!

Norman. Did you like my entrance? (*She turns, laughs a little, and moves to him.*)

Liz. Hi, Normal. I'm sorry. Are you all right?

Norman. I'm ok . . . Your marriage looks a little shaky. (*ELIZABETH half laughs and cries at the same time.*) You ok?

Liz. No.

Norman. I'm glad you're here.

Liz. I need a hug . . . Can I get a hug? (*NORMAN, still on the floor, his back against the wall, holds his arms out for her. She slips in easily. They hug.*) I always feel good when I'm with you. The only good thing about the last couple of years was meeting you. If you want to know Phil's best quality, it's you. (*She kisses him sweetly on the*

lips.) You really are the best friend I have in the whole world. Maybe the only friend. I don't want that to end with the marriage.
NORMAN. It won't.
LIZ. (*crying*) It will. I'll find some way to fuck it up like I fuck everything else up. You'll see.
NORMAN. Never happen.
LIZ. Promise?
NORMAN. Uh-huh.
LIZ. Say it.
NORMAN. Promise.
LIZ. (*LIZ breathes a sigh of relief.*) I feel better.
NORMAN. I love you, Elizabeth. I have for a while.
LIZ. Oh, Normal, how am I going to cover the overdraft?

BLACKOUT

SCENE 2

TIME: *Shortly thereafter.*
SETTING: *The Casino. At S.R. ELIZABETH is waiting impatiently, dressed as before. She is in "The Casino." Casino set is minimal. The sounds of the casino ring in the background.*

LIZ. C'mon, they're going to close in fifteen minutes. Hurry. (*NORMAN enters slightly out of breath, his jacket pockets bulging.*)
NORMAN. Sorry. I had to buy some chips and give Phil his toothbrush.
LIZ. How is he?
NORMAN. Not too bad.
LIZ. Shit. C'mon, let's play.

NORMAN. You're sure now? I could call your bank in the morning. We do a lot of business with them. They'll hold the overdraft.

LIZ. Will I have to pay them back?

NORMAN. When you have it.

LIZ. What's the good of that? I don't want to owe — didn't you teach me that?

NORMAN. Not exactly. I told you not to spend more than you make.

LIZ. Same thing. (*looks around*) C'mon. Let's not talk money. Let's make it. I want to play some craps. I want to roll dem bones. I'm betting the "come line." Watch out.

NORMAN. Let's play blackjack instead. You know how?

LIZ. I was born on a blackjack table.

NORMAN. (*gesturing toward tables*) Pick it.

LIZ. Consider it picked. (*She walks to table, her hand extended behind her for NORMAN to grab and follow. He does. She sits. He empties his pockets of chips on the table. LIZ gasps.*) How much are those?

NORMAN. Hundred dollars.

LIZ. (*gathering her arms around the chips*) All this is a hundred dollars?

NORMAN. Each. There are fifty of them.

LIZ. (*excited — putting them in piles*) Don't tell me. Fifty times a hundred . . . fifty times a hundred . . . I love making piles. I love watching them grow . . . Goddamn, Normal — how much we got here?

NORMAN. Five thousand. Make one pile.

LIZ. One pile? Gonna build me a mountain?

NORMAN. Go build a mountain. (*She begins making one pile.*)

Liz. How many of these cute little things we gonna bet?

Norman. The whole pile.

Liz. The whole pile? (*to the dealer*) Watch my pile. (*She gets up and walks away from the table, motions NORMAN to follow. He does.*) It's been a long day. I'm not sure I understood. You want me to bet $5000 on one hand?

Norman. Yes.

Liz. Honey, either you've had too much sun or you've spent too much time with your brother. I've always thought of you as the sane member of the family.

Norman. You want to cover the overdraft tomorrow without owing? We got ten minutes to closing. You want to gamble — let's gamble.

Liz. What happens if I lose?

Norman. You owe me and you owe the bank. Pay me after you pay them.

Liz. That's not all that's gonna happen . . . if I lose I'm going to take your left nut and squeeze it so hard your veins will pop out of your nose.

Norman. And if you win?

Liz. I'll do something equally dramatic.

Norman. Play the cards. (*She gives him a quick, nervous hug. Holding his hand, she returns to the table. With her free hand SHE moves the pile forward.*)

Liz. Deal.

(*They watch as the cards are drawn.*) Ten . . . one more ten . . . one more ten . . . ten. Ten — (*She moans and buries her head in NORMAN's stomach.*) Oh God, Normal — thirteen.

Norman. That's all right. He's showing a five. Just stick.

Liz. Just stick? With thirteen?

NORMAN. Just stick.

LIZ. (*to the dealer*) Hit me.

NORMAN. (*Throwing himself on the table, The chips flying.*) No. No play. She sticks. She sticks.

LIZ. Hit me. Hit me.

NORMAN. Time out. Time out. (*He grabs her from her seat. They move away for another conference.*)

LIZ. I am not sticking with thirteen.

NORMAN. He's showing a five.

LIZ. I don't care what he's showing. If I stick the only I can win is if he busts.

NORMAN. If you hit you can bust. That's the only advantage they have — if you bust and he busts you lose.

LIZ. If I lose at least I'll go out kicking and screaming — not laying down and dying.

NORMAN. Elizabeth, please — he's showing a five. Chances are he has fifteen. If he does, he has to hit. If he hits there's an excellent chance he's going to bust. Sometimes the right thing to do is do nothing. Let the other fellow make the mistake.

LIZ. (*long pause as she digests it*). . . Promise me I'm going to win.

NORMAN. I can't promise you you're going to win. I can promise you it's the right play. I can promise you if you make the right play often enough, in the long run you'll win.

LIZ. The long run. The long run for me is the next ten minutes.

NORMAN. The long run for both of us starts now. (*Short pause. She turns and heads back to table. He follows.*)

LIZ. (*to dealer*) Stick. (*They both watch as the dealer turns over his cards.*) Another five. He has ten. We're finished. I should've hit. I can't look. (*She buries her head in his stomach.*)

NORMAN. Four. He just pulled a four. He has fourteen.

LIZ. Four! I would've had seventeen. Oh, Normal.

NORMAN. Bust. Bust. Bust. Bust. (*Dealer takes another card.*) Eight! Eight and fourteen is how much! How much?!

LIZ. I don't know. I'm too nervous. How much?

NORMAN. Too much! Buuuuussted!

LIZ. (*looking up for the first time*) We won?

NORMAN. We won.

LIZ. (*turns to dealer and shouts*) Buuuuuussted! (*gets up, walks past NORMAN to* C.S., *dramatically turns to him and the table*) Piece of cake. (*They both laugh and move to each other. He spins her around.*)

NORMAN. (*to dealer*) Make out a cashier's check payable to the lady. We'll pick it up in the morning.

LIZ. (*to dealer*) Elizabeth — with a "Z." (*As they move* C.S. *lights dim on the casino. They are on the beach moving to hotel room.*) What would have happened? I would've hit the four — so I would have had seventeen. He hits the eight — he has eighteen. Oh, Normal, I'm glad we arrived at the right decision. So help me if God would've whispered "stick" I would've hit. How come I listen to you and nobody else? I have business managers, agents, ex-husband, present husband, and ever since I met you whenever I'm in a hole this voice cries out "Call Normal. Talk to Normal." You're so smart — how come?

NORMAN. Because you trust me. The real question is "How come you don't trust them?"

LIZ. Because they're full of shit. All of them. When times are good they can't be more helpful — and when

BE HAPPY FOR ME

they're not you can't find them. It's always "What's in it for me?" And I can understand that. I'm the same way. (*NORMAN starts to protest. She stops him.*) I am, Normal. Only more so.

NORMAN. Because you're frightened.

LIZ. Maybe. Doesn't matter. It's who I am. I'm comfortable with it. It becomes me. I'm not going to change. Darlin' when the rubber hits the road — right at that instant — it's "What's in it for me?" And it's the best goddamned question in the world. You know what scares me about us? I can't figure out what's in it for you.

NORMAN. That's easy. I love you.

LIZ. I know you do, Darlin'.

NORMAN. You don't. I'm not from California and I'm not in the theater. I don't use that word easily.

LIZ. (*kissing him sweetly*) You're very special.

NORMAN. You make me feel special. Young and alive and excited about who I am. Just walking down the street with you. The way you move. The way you sit. The way you laugh. What a wonderful laugh you have. You have a passion for life that's so appealing. so contagious—

LIZ. You're infected.

NORMAN. Only with you. I love you, Elizabeth. Honest and true.

LIZ. I'm glad. Makes me feel good.

NORMAN. Since the time we made love — I haven't thought of anything else.

LIZ. (*pulling away*) Since we what?

NORMAN. Made love.

LIZ. We made love?

NORMAN. Yes.

LIZ. We . . . You and me?

NORMAN. Yes . . . sort of.

Liz. What do you mean, "sort of"?

Norman. I can understand your not remembering. You had quite a bit to drink.

Liz. Oh, Normal . . . Are you going to turn out to be crazy like the rest of them?

Norman. No. I'm not crazy.

Liz. When was this? Where? How?

Norman. How? Well . . . you take a lady you're crazy about . . . a lady whose marriage is all but over to some opening night . . . and the party after . . . and then you take her to her hotel room because she's had some fight with her husband and won't sleep in the same house as he is.

Liz. Your house. (*He nods.*) And? . . .

Norman. And you talk a lot.

Liz. Yeh, I always wind up talking to you . . . so?

Norman. So . . . after a while you gave me this hug . . . I've never been hugged that way.

Liz. Yeah. I give good hugs. And?

Norman. And . . . you started unbuttoning my shirt and I started unbuttoning yours . . . And . . . you passed out.

Liz. That's it? . . . That's making love?

Norman. Sort of.

Liz. Sort of?

Norman. To me. I tucked you into bed . . . gave you a kiss on the cheek . . .

Liz. On the top of the head.

Norman. Yes, on the . . . you remember?

Liz. I didn't pass out. I got scared.

Norman. Scared?

Liz. You're a hell of a hugger too. I like crawling up to the edge. I don't like falling off.

Norman. You faked it? (*A steel band is heard playing*

some soft reggae. LIZ begins dancing to the music. NORMAN stares, transfixed.)

Liz. Don't look at me like I'm the one that's weird. It's you that's crazy, risking five grand trying to get me even.

Norman. You faked it!

Liz. You're the weirdest, sweetest man I know. I love you, Normal.

Norman. . . . You're so beautiful.

Liz. Dance. Dance with me.

Norman. I don't know how.

Liz. Just move . . . Move with me. (*He does. He's not bad.*) That's it . . . You feel it?

Norman. Yes. I feel it. It feels nice.

Liz. Slow and easy. That's it . . .

Norman. Look, Ma, I'm dancing.

Liz. Mmmnnn . . . that's nice. Oh God, you do feel nice. (*She rests her head on his shoulder, her arms around his neck, as they move to the music. The lights slowly fade.*)

BLACKOUT

Scene 3

Time: *The following morning.*
Setting: *As before. The hotel room. PHIL is seen slowly entering the hotel room. He looks tired and disheveled. A cigarette is behind his ear. He must have had quite a night. The noise of his clumsy entrance brings NORMAN in* s.l., *dressed in his bathing trunks, a robe and maroon loafers. They stare at one another for several beats.*

PHIL. I see you took to the shoes.
NORMAN. Yeah . . . for red they're not bad.
PHIL. You look ridiculous.
NORMAN. You're not looking too terrific either.
PHIL. Where were you? I waited with them at the bar for an hour. I left messages. I called the room.
NORMAN. I went to the casino.
PHIL. I know. For ten minutes. They you were supposed to meet me. I was stuck with both of them all night long.
NORMAN. What happened?
PHIL. What happened? I had to fuck them both.
NORMAN. I'm sorry.
PHIL. I'm not as young as I used to be.
NORMAN. What am I apologizing for? You had as many women in one night as I did in my entire life—
PHIL. Wasn't that what we were supposed to do. I was doing it for you.
NORMAN. I'm sorry. I'm sorry I stuck you.
PHIL. I didn't fuck them both. I barely had the strength to talk to them both—waiting up all night for you. They think I'm Mr. Sensitivity. (*moving to his bedroom*) I'm exhausted. I'm going to sleep.
NORMAN. Don't go in there. Please. (*PHIL turns to him.*) She's asleep.
PHIL. (*moving to phone*) I'm calling security. I'm going to get her ass out of here. (*gazes on NORMAN's perfectly made bed*) Where did you sleep? (*NORMAN doesn't answer. PHIL, aware now:*) Say it ain't so, mister.
NORMAN. I can't. I don't know what to say.
PHIL. Tell me you couldn't help it. She threw herself at you. It was one brief moment—a fleeting instant—that's all. Means nothing. Practice on me what you're

BE HAPPY FOR ME 51

going to tell Myra . . . Good going, brother — you got the hat trick. My wife on my bed on my vacation. Congratulations.

NORMAN. Your marriage is over. You sat here yesterday—

PHIL. I don't care about her. She could've screwed the lifeguard as far as I'm concerned.

NORMAN. They don't have lifeguards in the Caribbean.

PHIL. You're my brother.

NORMAN. I love her, Phil. I have for a while.

PHIL. Oh, great . . . a roll in the hay ain't enough . . . now it's love. Was that the first time?

NORMAN. . . . Sort of.

PHIL. What do you mean, "sort of"?

NORMAN. It was. It was the first time.

PHIL. What do you mean, "loved her for a while"? While we were still living together?

NORMAN. Probably. I didn't know it at the time.

PHIL. So all this sweet brother-in-law bullshit — let me take you here — let me take you there — let me help . . . was just an excuse to get in her pants. Wasn't it? Huh — wasn't it?

NORMAN. It was being nice. It seems to me I've spent my life being nice to everybody.

PHIL. Except maybe me and Myra.

NORMAN. I wanted to tell you. That was my reason for this trip. I didn't know this was going to happen.

PHIL. Oh, now I get it. That's why you dragged me down here. You were going to break it to me gently. Day one, "I'm in love with love." Day two, "Actually, it's someone you know." Day three, "By the way, it happens to be your wife." Day four, "Time to go home." Perfect.

Nice and easy, like a good tan. Except it's not nice and it's not easy. It's my wife, brother. My wife.

NORMAN. Stop it. Your ex-wife. It's tough enough.

PHIL. Tough enough for who? What makes you think it's easier the third time? It hurts more.

NORMAN. Remember, on the beach when we talked about what I wanted—

PHIL. Yeah, I know. The banjo on one knee and my wife on the other.

NORMAN. About the pitter pat. About being alive. That's the way I am with her. Phil, it's like I've lived my whole life inside a plastic bubble. I could look out and see what was happening; smile, nod, comment, and never be touched. Never.

PHIL. You didn't get touched—you got laid.

NORMAN. I didn't get laid. I got a new life.

PHIL. You got laid. I got fucked. (*PHIL throws himself on bed face down. NORMAN goes over trying to comfort him. Like a child PHIL shrugs him off. NORMAN takes two steps back.*)

NORMAN. Do you want me to go . . . I'll leave if you want me to.

PHIL. (*muffled—face down on bed*) Do whatever the hell you want. (*NORMAN begins to exit* S.L., *toward ELIZABETH's room.*) What do you want me to say? What do you want me to do?

NORMAN. I want you to be happy for me. Last night was the best night of my entire life.

PHIL. Oh God . . .

NORMAN. Phil, I even danced. Me! The guy whose wedding had to be postponed three months because I broke Myra's foot practicing the waltz. I did the reggae, Phil. Only blacks do the reggae. You should have been there—you'd have been proud of me.

PHIL. He never stops.

NORMAN. And it was easy. Everything was easy and exciting and wonderful. If you love me be happy for me. I never intended to hurt you. Don't make me feel bad for feeling so good.

PHIL. You're some piece of work, mister. I always knew you were the best. Always said so. But I can't believe you're this good. I can't believe you're making me feel guilty because you fucked my wife.

NORMAN. I didn't. Stop saying that. I didn't.

PHIL. You didn't? What did you do?

NORMAN. I slept with her.

PHIL. Excuse me . . .

NORMAN. I don't mean "slept" like you mean "slept." I mean literally. And only for the last hour.

PHIL. You actually slept?

NORMAN. I was exhausted, Phil.

PHIL. What did you do before—while I was waiting for you at the bar . . . while we were on vacation?

NORMAN. Talked mostly. Held hands. Laughed. Cried. Hugged a lot. It was wonderful. It was a magic night.

PHIL. . . . You didn't fuck her? You laid next to her on the bed all night long and you didn't?

NORMAN. No.

PHIL. I don't believe you.

NORMAN. I didn't.

PHIL. Why not?

NORMAN. Well . . . you know me and deferred gratification.

PHIL. Yeah, I know. Ridiculous question. Just trying to make conversation.

NORMAN. I love her, Phil.

PHIL. Was she wearing old number 8?

NORMAN. I'm trying to tell you something.

PHIL. I'm trying to ask you something. Was she wearing old number 8?

NORMAN. No.

PHIL. Bullshit. Bullshit. She was. I know.

NORMAN. She wasn't wearing anything.

PHIL. Nice. Very nice.

NORMAN. What do you want me to say?

PHIL. Break it to me gently. Don't tell me a sweatshirt and jogging pants. I won't buy it. How about a bikini? She has a lot of bikinis.

NORMAN. She wore a bikini.

PHIL. Really . . . which one?

NORMAN. . . . I don't know.

PHIL. C'mon. What color?

NORMAN. . . . Phil.

PHIL. What color!

NORMAN. Flesh tone.

PHIL. Why are you doing this to me?

NORMAN. Because you're being ridiculous.

PHIL. I'm being ridiculous. I'm being ridiculous!

NORMAN. Ridiculous. What else would you call it— asking me to defend the fact that I didn't have intercourse with your wife last night?

PHIL. Of course. I'm being ridiculous. This is said to me by the same person whose dick becomes . . . (*motioning with widespread hands*) . . . this long when he sees a hairy schlub on the beach with a dick (*motioning with thumb and forefinger*) this long. And this same person expects me to believe he spent the night in bed with a flesh toned Elizabeth without ever—Why didn't you screw her?

NORMAN. Because I don't need that! I need to be in love. I thought I told you.

BE HAPPY FOR ME

PHIL. I see. You did it to prove a point?

NORMAN. Did what?

PHIL. I'm sorry. You didn't do it to prove a point — to prove you're right?

NORMAN. I don't know what's right. I didn't do it because I couldn't. I couldn't without talking to you — without talking to Myra.

PHIL. You looking for our permission? You don't have it. Myra and I don't consent.

NORMAN. I need you. You said I never needed you. I need you now. This is unchartered water for me. Help me work it through with a minimum of pain for everyone.

PHIL. Help you work through what?

NORMAN. I love her. I want to be with her. I want that more than anything. Help me find the way. Please.

PHIL. If I can accept this . . . if I can work it through in my own head . . . if I . . . somehow work it through, we're even. Before tonight I owed you everything. You're calling in all your chits. If I accept this, the slate is clean. Deal?

NORMAN. You never owed me anything.

PHIL. Deal?

NORMAN. Deal. (*PHIL, in a rush of emotion, pulls his brother into his arms, stays, then pulls away.*)

PHIL. . . . Does she love you?

NORMAN. She says she does.

PHIL. Says she does. You know what she loves? Jaguars, margaritas, the wind in her hair. Loves it. Loves it all. But she doesn't love people. She doesn't know how.

NORMAN. I love her enough for both of us.

PHIL. You're talking like an infant. Do you know what she'll do to you? She'll kill you. She'll chew you up and spit you out so fast you won't know what's happening.

You're going in prime sirloin and within a month you'll be stew meat.

NORMAN. I won't. I won't let that happen. I'm not part of the stew. I know she can be outrageous. I don't mind. The more outrageous she is the better I like it.

PHIL. Except when it's directed toward you. You're good but no one is that good they can make people change. She doesn't love you. She doesn't love anyone. She loves what you are to her — maybe.

NORMAN. I don't want to argue with you. I want you to help me.

PHIL. Help you what? Kill yourself? What are you doing? You got a wonderful wife — great kids — position — money — the whole package. My whole life I'm looking for what you have. What are you doing? (*NORMAN starts to answer.*) Listen — before you say anything I want to put a condition on the rest of this vacation. I am now going to speak to you as a lawyer, not a brother. Say whatever you want but if you mention the word marriage — to anyone — I'm going out that door and you'll never see me again as long as you live. This is not the 50's. You kiss her — you're not engaged. You hug her she don't get the tombstone next door. Agreed? . . . Ok. Now I'm about to tell you something that if you live to be a hundred, God forbid, you'll never hear better advice said in a clearer way. Listen. Are you listening?

NORMAN. I'm listening.

PHIL. Stay married. Fuck around. It's cheaper.

NORMAN. Words to live by.

PHIL. They should be etched in the tablets they're so good.

NORMAN. All right. Help me find a way to be with her

BE HAPPY FOR ME 57

and stay married. I'll do it.

PHIL. Don't forget—I'm saying this as your lawyer, not your brother . . . Ok? Take a leave. Take a leave from Morgan and take a leave from Myra. Say three months. You shouldn't have too much problem with Morgan.

NORMAN. I could work that out with Morgan. No problem.

PHIL. You could work it out with Myra too. It'll be a little harder but you could do it. The timing is right. Pop just died. Give her some of your middle-aged "I got to find myself" bullshit. You got fifty years together. She might not like it, but where's she going? Knowing her she'll probably help you pack and drive you to the airport.

NORMAN. Ok. Done. Then what?

PHIL. Tell her you're staying with me. I'm all alone with four bedrooms. Elizabeth lives fifteen minutes away in Malibu. Go sip margaritas with her. Call in daily for your messages. You might last three weeks—if she goes easy on you. I'm really starting to feel like the heavy here. Even the Romans didn't throw Jews to the lions. (*NORMAN slowly begins to smile. It's a big smile. It's a workable plan. In fact, it's perfect.*) I don't believe I'm doing this.

NORMAN. (*exultant, his arm around his brother, kisses him on the cheek*) Perfect. Perfect. And you'll see. It's won't be bad. In fact, it's part of our tradition—our heritage.

PHIL. What are you talking about?

NORMAN. It's even written about in the Bible. When one brother can't make it with his wife, it's expected the other brother should take her unto himself. I swear to

you—it's in the Talmud.
PHIL. Not if he "can't make it." If he dies, asshole!

(*On the word "asshole" ELIZABETH enters from PHIL's room fully dressed. Carrying suitcases she puts suitcases down. Long pause, as the three stare at each other.*)

LIZ. Talk about pregnant pauses.
NORMAN. Good morning.
LIZ. (*to NORMAN*) Good morning. (*to PHIL*) Good morning. You're not talking to me anymore?
PHIL. You have a good time in my bed last night?
LIZ. A lot better than when you were in it. (*PHIL, hysterical, screams and rushes toward her. NORMAN, with much effort, attempts to restrain him.*)
PHIL. I'm going to kill her. I'm going to fucking kill her. Why do you want to be with her? She's fucking crazy. Let me go!
LIZ. I'm crazy? You're crazier. You married me. Let him go.
PHIL. I'm crazy. Really! Did you tell him? Did you? Did you tell him you wanted me to sue myself to get you a better deal?
LIZ. No, I didn't. Did you tell him I offered you one-third of what I got? No, I'm sure you didn't tell him that! (*NORMAN and PHIL stop struggling, stunned by LIZ's logic. PHIL, disgusted, walks away.*)
PHIL. (*to NORMAN*) I can't be with her. I'll be on the beach. When she leaves let me know. If she stays I'm checking out.
LIZ. Don't' go far. I'm leaving. I already called for the cab.

PHIL. You should never have come. (*PHIL, tired, his fury spent, starts toward her, stops in disgust and exits to the beach.*)

NORMAN. That was unnecessary.

LIZ. I don't care. I hate him. Don't lecture me.

NORMAN. I care. He's my brother and I love him. That won't make it any easier.

LIZ. (*takes a big sigh and silently nods her assent*) Can I start again? Good morning, darling.

NORMAN. Good morning, darling. (*They kiss.*)

LIZ. When he gets back to L.A., I'll send him some flowers and a little note.

NORMAN. Thank you.

LIZ. Don't thank me. You're paying for the flowers. (*kisses him again*)

NORMAN. Don't go.

LIZ. I have to. I told you last night.

NORMAN. Just one more day? We have so much to talk about.

LIZ. We'll talk. Where's the fire? Didn't you tell me about how the long run begins now--that we got the rest of our lives, huh? Was I hallucinating?

NORMAN. Are you going to quote me the rest of our lives?

LIZ. Only if you love me for the rest of our lives. (*He smiles and hugs her.*) And only when it suits my purpose.

NORMAN. Let me go with you.

LIZ. I think you should be with Phil. He needs you now.

NORMAN. You're being considerate of Phil?

LIZ. See the effect you have on me. One night with you and shazaam—Miss Congeniality. (*We hear a horn beep.*) I've go to go. That's the cab.

NORMAN. Let me go with you. It'll just take a few minutes to change.

Liz. No.

Norman. Why?

Liz. Why? You don't smoke. I can't stand being with people who don't smoke. They're constantly waving . . . (*demonstrates as if waving smoke away*) . . . their hand in my face.

Norman. I can learn again. It's like riding a bike — you never forget. Give me a cigarette.

Liz. Stop it.

Norman. Stop what? I love you. I want to be with you.

Liz. No.

Norman. Why? At least give me a reason.

Liz. Because the homes I break up are generally my own.

Norman. You're not breaking up anyone's home. I just want to be with you longer.

Liz. I know what you want. I know you. Don't love me so much.

Norman. . . . I can't help it.

Liz. Oh God, Normal . . . please. I'm so crazy as it is.

Norman. Don't stop me. I love you. I love you. I can't stop saying it.

Liz. Oh Normal . . . please . . . I need you so much. It would be so easy for me. I'd say "yes" and I wouldn't have to worry about another thing for the rest of my life. Whatever I'd do you'd always be there trailing behind with that — What do they call it? — pooper dooper — cleaning up the mess. Wouldn't you?

Norman. I'd try.

Liz. Try? You'd do it. You do it now. Who'd be there to pick up your mess?

Norman. I wouldn't need anyone. I'd have you.

Liz. You wouldn't have me. I'd lose you. Look at your

BE HAPPY FOR ME 61

brother. I'll make you crazy. I've already made you crazy.

NORMAN. No, I go through life always doing the right thing. Always watching the revolution from hotel windows. My kids are great. My wife is respectable. My job is secure. My investments are sound. I've never even been sick. I got it all save up for you.

LIZ. What are you talking about?

NORMAN. I'm talking about us. I don't care if you're crazy. I don't care if I'm crazy. I care about you. I care about being with you. (*Horn sounds again.*) Shut the hell up!

LIZ. Normal, listen. You don't know. Ssshh. You don't. You are talking to an actress — not a star — not an entertainer — not with big tits and a phony smile — an actress. And the only time I'm alive is when the hush begins and the curtain goes up. When I have that in my live I don't need you — I don't need anyone. And when that's not happening you don't want to know me. You'd be walking naked into a buzzsaw with your twig stuck out. Zzaap! (*NORMAN turns away, trying to find the right words.*) Don't be angry with me. Please? I'm trying to keep you, not lose you.

NORMAN. I'm not angry. I'm confused. I don't understand why you won't even give it a try. Not even a try? Let me come with you. Please. It's as close to begging as I've ever gotten.

LIZ. Stop it. You can't come.

NORMAN. Why? For God's sake why!?!

LIZ. Because I am getting married next month. Because my intended — love that word — will be there. Because he might not appreciate your slobbering all over me. All right? Are you happy now? (*NORMAN moves away.*) You want all the gory details? (*NORMAN shakes his head "no".*) Tough. I love you and you're going to hear them. (*Horn sounds again.*) The gentleman said shut the hell up! So shut the hell up! Don't shut me out. I shared everything with you when I was married. I can at least share with you when I'm engaged. (*He doesn't react.*) You used to have a good sense of humor.

NORMAN. So last night signified nothing.

LIZ. You want to know what last night signified? It signified when I'm hot I'm hot, and when I'm not I'm not. Last night I was hot—and you blew it . . . His name is McDonald. He's thirty years older than me—and he's very rich.

NORMAN. What is he—a farmer?

LIZ. A farmer?

NORMAN. Old McDonald had a farm.

LIZ. Oy-veh, you really are losing your sense of humor. He's not a farmer. He made it in oil, gas and real estate.

NORMAN. The usual shit.

LIZ. Only met him a few months ago. Worships me, would you believe? Comes from a little town outside of Atlanta. Cute place called Lithonia. The truth, wouldn't you love to be from Lith-oown-yah. (*She laughs.*) He has a house in Malibu. Likes to talk about the south a lot.

NORMAN. You'd rather discuss oil and gas.

LIZ. Exactly.

NORMAN. Do you love him?

LIZ. Very good. Took a long time to ask that.

NORMAN. Do you?

LIZ. I'm tired of love. I'm tired of the way it ends.

NORMAN. Why him? Why some farmer you hardly know?

LIZ. Because he's sweet and rich and crazy about me. And I don't think it's the worst thing in the world entering a marriage with dry pants on. I tried it the other way—it doesn't work.

NORMAN. You're quitting. You're giving up.

LIZ. I'm not. I'm trading. I'm trading hot pants for cold cash. I'm trading love for freedom. Wait till I tell you. You're going to be so excited for me. No, I want you to guess. C'mon, guess what I'm getting for a wedding present? . . . You'll never guess. "The Elizabeth Gorney Center for the Performing Arts—at Lithonia." Sound nice? Got the architect's picture of what it's going to look like as an engagement present. The man sure do know how to close a deal. "The Elizabeth Gorney Center for the Performing Arts—at Lithonia." Got a nice ring to it. A little like "The University of California—at Berkeley." Sounds the same, doesn't it? C'mon, doesn't it?

NORMAN. Exactly the same.

LIZ. I'll make it sound better. Ten million bucks. That's what it's costing. Ten big ones. It's going to have two theaters: one in the round, one proscenium. Not bad for a "goil" from Joisey City, huh? I can be like Burt Reynolds. He's got something like that in Florida. Except I'll be richer—and taller. C'mon. What do you think? Honest.

NORMAN. . . . I'm delighted.

LIZ. Oh, Normal, please mean that. Say it like you mean it.

NORMAN. What do you want from me? What do you want me to say? Great?

LIZ. It's my dream come true. These could be the best years of my life. I want you to be happy for me. If you love me I want you to be happy for me.

NORMAN. (*Stares at her as the sound of his own words come back at him.*) I want to ask you something. Be honest with me. Promise?

Liz. I never lied to you. I won't start now. You're probably the only person I never lied to.

Norman. Ok. Close your eyes and let's play "pretend." Can you do that?

Liz. Better than anything else. (*She closes her eyes.*) Ready.

Norman. Let's pretend the farmer proposed but you said you'd let him know. You with me?

Liz. With you.

Norman. Good. Now let's pretend I said, "I want to start a life with you. Start a life with you, and if it goes as good as I think it will, as I know it will, we can spend the rest of our lives together." You still with me? (*Her eyes closed, she nods "yes".*) Good. Now I say to you, "Please give it a try. I can't make you a theater but I can make you happy." Now open your eyes. (*She does.*) What do you say?

Liz. I want to marry him and call you. (*NORMAN turns away.*) Don't turn away from me. I need you. I don't know if this is going to work. Who knows? What's forever? What's even real?

Norman. I'm real.

Liz. Yes. You're real. Last night was real. Right now all I've got is a picture and a promise. I've been there before. You're more important to me than him or anyone, and all kinds of people will come and go in my life but you'll always be there.

Norman. In my life people don't come and go. They come and stay.

Liz. That's what makes you so special. That's what makes your love for me so special. I know you're going to be there. And I know if you're there everything else is possible . . . maybe not possible . . . but easier. And

BE HAPPY FOR ME

listen to me, shithead — you need me too. Who else can you talk to like you can talk to me, huh? . . . Huh?

NORMAN. No one.

LIZ. You're darn tootin', no one. You're always going to be a part of my life — even if I have to pretend. Now are you going to keep your promise to me or am I going to have to pretend?

NORMAN. (*turning to her for the first time*) . . . Since when did you become so articulate?

LIZ. (*almost crying*) Survival . . . I'm almost as good at survival as I am at Let's pretend.

NORMAN. I love you.

LIZ. No matter what?

NORMAN. No matter what. (*They move to each other and embrace.*)

LIZ. And you know something else — 'bout getting hot and all? Runs in cycles. No promises but if you hang in you might catch the next one.

NORMAN. Is it like Halley's Comet. Will I have to wait another forty-nine years?

LIZ. . . . Sort of. (*They hug and squeeze. He kisses her hard. She holds the kiss several beats, then breaks it off, moves away.*) I got to go. I miss my plane I've had it. I'se headed for Lithonia. The closing on the land. I got three lawyers, an architect — even the mayor. Probably some press. Lawyer called just before I left. Said we have to make an — think I remember? . . . Oh yeah — an Environmental Impact Statement. What the hell do I say?

NORMAN. Tell them it's your environment. You just paid for it. Tell them to get the hell off your land.

LIZ. Perfect. That's exactly what I'm going to say. How come you're not a press agent? (*They both laugh, NORMAN kind of weakly. She moves, suitcase in hand, to exit.*) You and your brother are some pair. One's into impotence. The other's into abstinence. (*NORMAN laughs.*) How come you always laugh at my jokes . . . (*She exits, sees PHIL, shouts to him.*) You can go in now. I'm leaving. Oh, by the way, I'm getting married. If I need a pre-nuptial you're representing me. (*turns to stage exit and sees cabbie, who has just appeared*) Come on. Let's go. I'm late. Put a move on. (*She exits. PHIL, frantic, runs back to the room. NORMAN sits on bed.*)

PHIL. You promised me, damnit. You promised me!

NORMAN. What are you talking about?

PHIL. You promised me you wouldn't even use the word marriage. Promised.

NORMAN. I didn't.

PHIL. She told me she was getting married.

NORMAN. Not to me. Some other guy. Next month.

PHIL. Oh, thank God . . . (*breathes a sigh of relief*) . . . I'm sorry . . . look, it's the best thing. Let her be someone else's headache . . . did you say next month?

NORMAN. Yes.

PHIL. You're sure?

NORMAN. That's what she said.

PHIL. (*jumping up and down with glee*) Attaway . . . attaway . . . Fantastic. My payments stop when she marries. I don't think she knows. I'm going to save fifty grand. Fifty grand. Norm — fifty fucking grand. Maybe forty-five. I got to check the chart. The boys at Morgan Guaranty are going to be proud of me. C'mon. Don't be depressed. Cheer up. I just made fifty grand. Be happy for me. (*NORMAN begins to laugh. He becomes slightly hysterical.*) Will you let me in on it?

NORMAN. What am I going to do with the feelings,

Phil? How do I deal with that? What do I do with them?

PHIL. You're in great shape. You have the package. All you're missing is the ribbon. Come here. C'mon. C'mon. I want to show you something. (*NORMAN rises. PHIL puts one arm around his brother's shoulder and walks him toward the beach.*) Look out there. Look at all the ribbons. The only thing is, you can't have the ribbon on the package. You can have the ribbon alongside the package. So what's so terrible? It's not worth getting depressed about.

NORMAN. It's the most depressing thing I ever heard.

PHIL. It's not. Try it. It's as good as it gets.

NORMAN. I want the ribbon *on* the package.

PHIL. You can't have it. It doesn't stay. The whole thing always unravels. The only question is when.

NORMAN. . . . You don't believe that?

PHIL. Believe it? I make a hell of a living because of it. How many people you know have both? (*NORMAN stares at him, unable to answer. PHIL smiles sadly.*) I didn't know we hung out in the same crowd. C'mon. Let's get some breakfast. I'm starved.

NORMAN. I can't go this way. I look ridiculous.

PHIL. In fact, let me buy you a goddamned beach wardrobe. It's about time. My treat. I just made fifty grand. (*almost at exit*) C'mon. C'mon. We're on vacation. Let's get us a wardrobe, some breakfast and some ribbons. C'mon. (*PHIL exits. NORMAN is alone onstage. Pause several beats. NORMAN sits quietly, head in hands, on side of bed. PHIL reenters, moves quickly to him on bed.*) C'mon. You'll feel better once you get something to eat.

NORMAN. I'm sorry I cause you such . . . I'm sorry.

PHIL. They have bagels here. Flown in daily from Miami. A toasted bagel is good for the soul.

NORMAN. I'll get a shirt. (*He exits.*)

PHIL. Attaboy. I didn't even know she was seeing anybody. Who is he?

NORMAN. (*offstage*) I don't know. Some rich farmer from Georgia. He's going to build her a theater.

PHIL. A theater?

NORMAN. (*offstage*) A wedding present.

PHIL. Oh God. Don't tell me. In Lithonia?

NORMAN. (*enters*) How did you know?

PHIL. Easy come. Easy go. Shit.

NORMAN. Phil . . . What's going on?

PHIL. She lied to you.

NORMAN. No.

PHIL. She lied to you. There is no theater. There is no marriage.

NORMAN. No. I know when someone's lying. She had all the details. She didn't even want to tell me.

PHIL. She's an actress, remember?

NORMAN. Phil, stop it. She wouldn't lie to me. I'm the only person she never lied to.

PHIL. Never lied, huh? How's this sound? "I'm trading. I'm trading hot pants for cold cash." (*NORMAN sits, stunned.*) It comes from a shit little play she was rehearsing when I met her. I used to have to sit there and listen to her practice those bullshit lines. Called *Lady from Lithonia*. About as many people saw her do it then as saw her do it now. It opened and closed in one night. It's her favorite play. She lied to you. Welcome to the real world.

NORMAN. . . . Why?

PHIL. . . . Normie.

NORMAN. Why would she do that?

PHIL. Why? Wake up, will you? How about it's Elizabeth being Elizabeth. Keeping you where she wants to keep you. Using you where she wants to use you. (*Nor-

man buries his head in his hands.) C'mon, let's get something to eat.

NORMAN. You go. I'd like to be alone for a while.

PHIL. Normie, we're on vacation. Normie, please? . . . Look, I don't have to be right. I might not be the most objective person in the world when it comes to Elizabeth. There are other possibilities.

NORMAN. I asked her to stay. She said, "I know you. Don't love me so much." Did that come from the play?

PHIL. No. In the play she gets her theatre built and lives happily ever after.

NORMAN. I said I'd go with her. She said, "No. I'm trying to keep you, not lose you."

PHIL. She said that?

NORMAN. Yes. Why?

PHIL. Maybe she's smarter than you are. Why does everyone get so smart after they leave me?

NORMAN. I don't understand.

PHIL. You don't understand? I told you there were other possibilities. Look, I don't want to blow your cover Mr. Self Restraint. Mr. I don't need that. "I need to be in love." I don't care what you need. Saying no to Elizabeth in the sack is like saying no to St. Peter at the Pearly Gates. It's theoretically possible—it's just not done. When it was good for us—she was the best.

NORMAN. What are you saying?

PHIL. Look at it logically. Where is she going? Back to an empty house and unemployment? If you think she needed you when we were married, wait till you see how much she needs you now. That's why she came down here—to insure that. She sleeps with you, it's better than insurance. It's money in the bank. But she didn't. Therefore, a case could be made that she was trying to protect you.

NORMAN. From what?

PHIL. From following your dick—like the rest of us. Look at you. You're a pussycat. You'd do anything. Give up everything you ever worked for. If you were a poet, you'd say it was the most loving thing she's ever done.

NORMAN. Do you believe that?

PHIL. I'm not a poet.

NORMAN. She thinks it wouldn't work. She agrees with you. She really does love me. She left me because she loves me. She's just trying to protect me. That's her way of protecting me. That's her way of loving me.

PHIL. It's possible. It doesn't make any difference. It all ends the same. She's there and you're here—thank God. You see, it really doesn't matter.

NORMAN. It does matter. To me it matters. She left me because she loves me. It's there. It's attainable.

PHIL. In our lifetime?

NORMAN. Oh yes, Yes. In our lifetime. There's hope for me. For you, for all of us.

PHIL. . . . Even you and Myra?

NORMAN. . . . You know for a divorce lawyer you're a hell of a brother.

PHIL. It took me a while, but I'm getting there.

NORMAN. Thank you, Phil.

PHIL. Don't change the subject. There's hope for you and Myra?

NORMAN. I don't know. Elizabeth taught me to reggae. And now that I can do the reggae, everything is possible.

PHIL. Everything?

NORMAN. Yes, everything.

PHIL. Even breakfast?

NORMAN. Even breakfast.

PHIL. Good. I hate that shirt.

NORMAN. Let me ask you a question. Are you still buying me that beach wardrobe?

PHIL. If I don't starve to death first. Are you still springing for breakfast?

NORMAN. Sure. About that beach wardrobe—I want the kind with thongs.

PHIL. Thongs? What about the thing that goes between your toes? Doesn't it hurt?

NORMAN. Hurt? Are you kidding? Piece of cake. (*They laugh. NORMAN puts his arm around his brother. They exit.*)

CURTAIN

PROPERTY PLOT

ACT I, Scene 1

2 beach chairs
fashionable canvas beach bag containing:
   2 large towels
   1 small towel
   1 screw-top medicine bottle w/liquid
   1 spoon
   other lotions, unguents, salves & jellies
beach umbrella
thermos bottle
sunglasses (PHIL)

ACT I, Scene 2

1 screw-top medicine bottle
1 spoon
several bottles of pills
various colognes, men's accessories
1 glass of water
phone
ashtray
lint brush
2 pieces of luggage
checkbook
cigarettes
cigarette lighter

ACT II, Scene 1

cigarettes
cigarette lighter
styrofoam coffee cup

ACT II, Scene 2

50 gambling chips
playing cards (pre-arranged as indicated in scene)

ACT II, Scene 3

cigarettes
cigarette lighter
luggage (same as ACT I, Scene 2)

COSTUME PLOT

ACT I, Scene 1

PHIL
floral print shirt
jogging pants
brief bathing suit

NORMAN
blue floral print shirt
matching shorts
black over the calf socks
black laced shoes
pale blue hat

ACT I, Scene 2

NORMAN
charcoal suit
black laced shoes
white shirt
maroon tie
(change into)
— maroon sports jacket
  maroon loafers

PHIL
navy double breasted blazer
medium blue tropical shirt
cream slacks
medium brown shoes

LIZ
yellow dress with halter top and wrap around jacket
yellow and black shoes

ACT II, Scene 1

NORMAN, PHIL and *LIZ* same as ACT I, Scene 2

ACT II, Scene 2

LIZ and *NORMAN* same as before

ACT II, Scene 3

PHIL
same as ACT II, Scene 1, but disheveled

NORMAN
charcoal pants
maroon loafers
medium grey robe

LIZ
Purple skirt
purple print blouse
matching shoes

SOUND PLOT

Pre-show, post-show and segue music consists of popular standards synthesized with mock-Caribbean rhythmic accents, in the manner of a tropical cocktail lounge.

ACT I, Scene 1 begins with the sound of pounding surf and occasional screeching seagulls.

ACT II, Scene 2 begins with ambient casino noise and segues into quiet surf with the action of the scene.

ACT II, Scene 3 requires three increasingly impatient off-stage taxi horns.

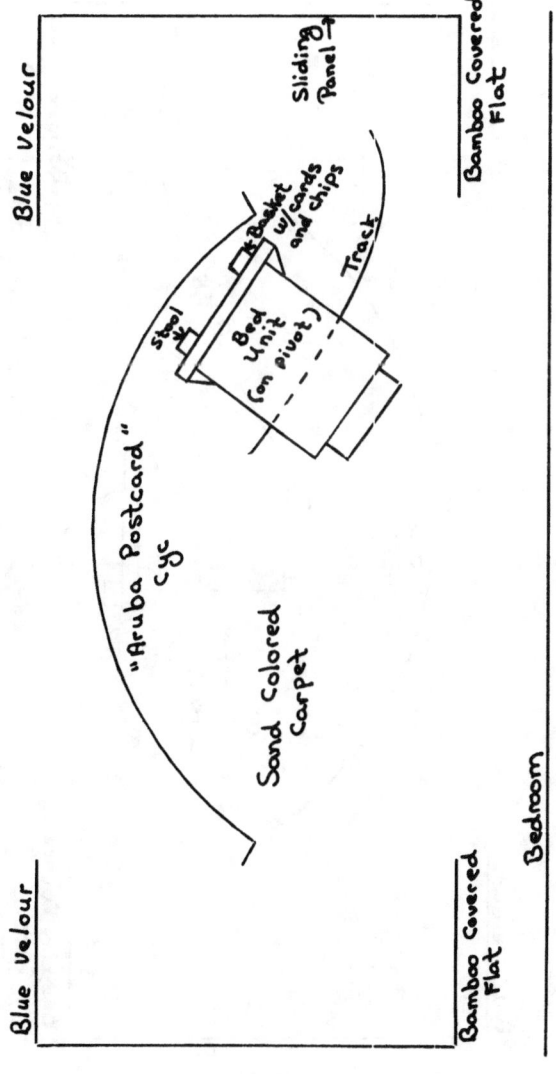

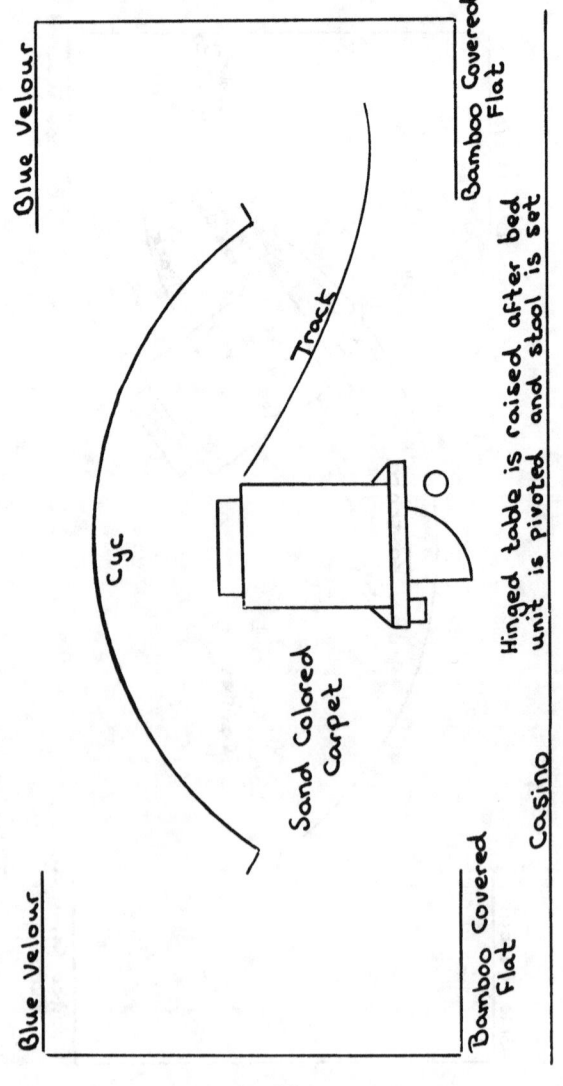

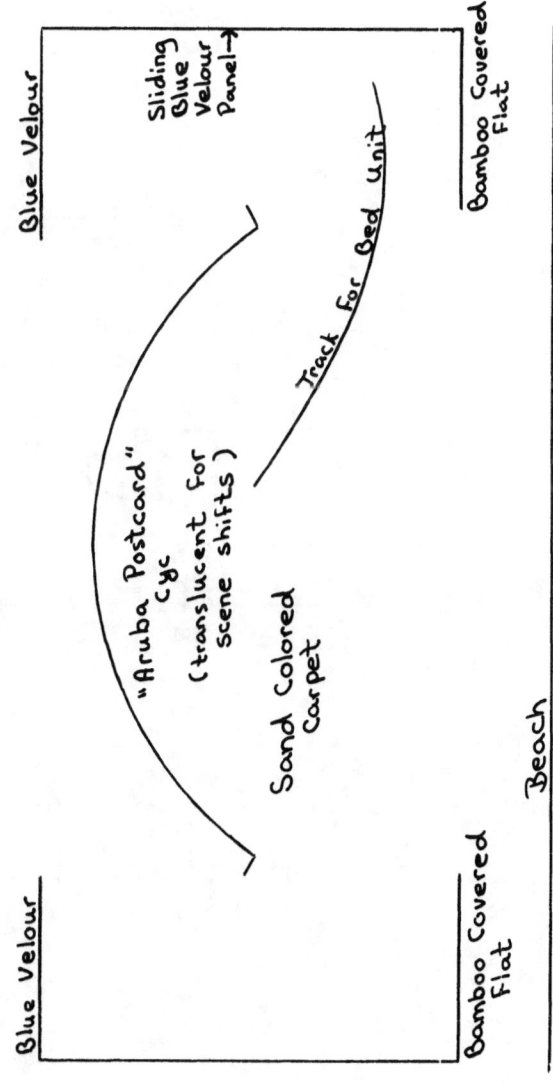

www.ingramcontent.com/pod-product-compliance
Lightning Source LLC
Chambersburg PA
CBHW070647300426
44111CB00013B/2316